THE VERY BEST OF Prince

ISBN 978-1-4950-8923-7

HAL•LEONARD®

7777 W. BLUEMOUND RD. P.O. BOX 13819 MILWAUKEE, WI 53213

In Australia Contact:
Hal Leonard Australia Pty. Ltd.
4 Lentara Court
Cheltenham, Victoria, 3192 Australia
Email: ausadmin@halleonard.com.au

Visit Hal Leonard Online at
www.halleonard.com

Alphabet Street

Words and Music by Prince

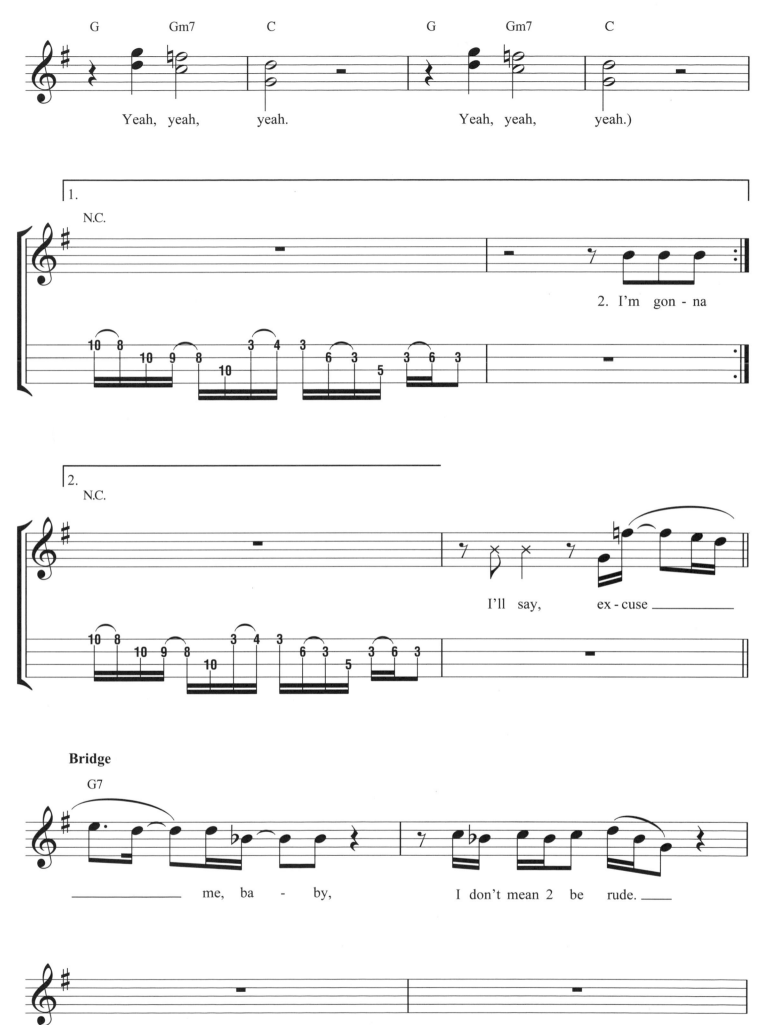

if U don't mind, I would like 2...　　　　　　　　　　watch...

(Yeah,　yeah,　　　yeah.)　　　　　　Can I? _____ (Yeah,　yeah,

yeah.　　　　　　　　　　Yeah,　yeah,　　　yeah.)

3. We're　go - in'

down,　down,　down　　　if　that's　the　on - ly　way ____ 2　make　this

cruel, cruel world hear what we've got to say. ____

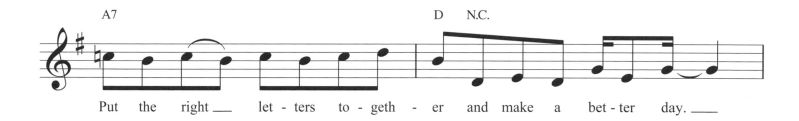

Put the right ____ let - ters to - geth - er and make a bet - ter day. ____

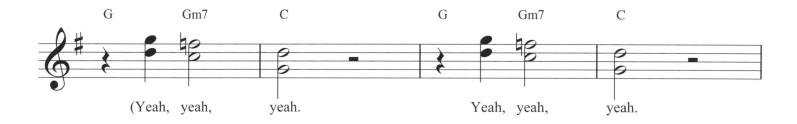

(Yeah, yeah, yeah. Yeah, yeah, yeah.

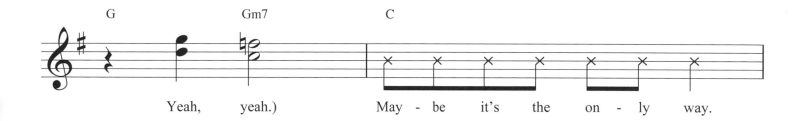

Yeah, yeah.) May - be it's the on - ly way.

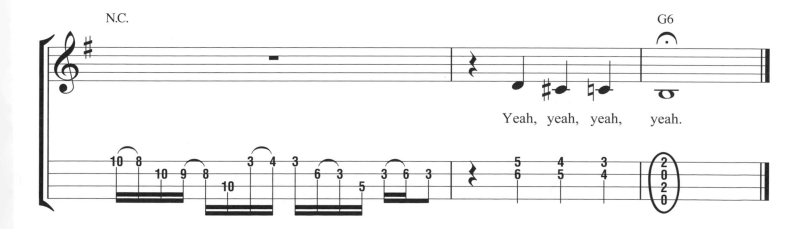

Yeah, yeah, yeah, yeah.

Cream

Words and Music by Prince

Diamonds and Pearls

Words and Music by Prince

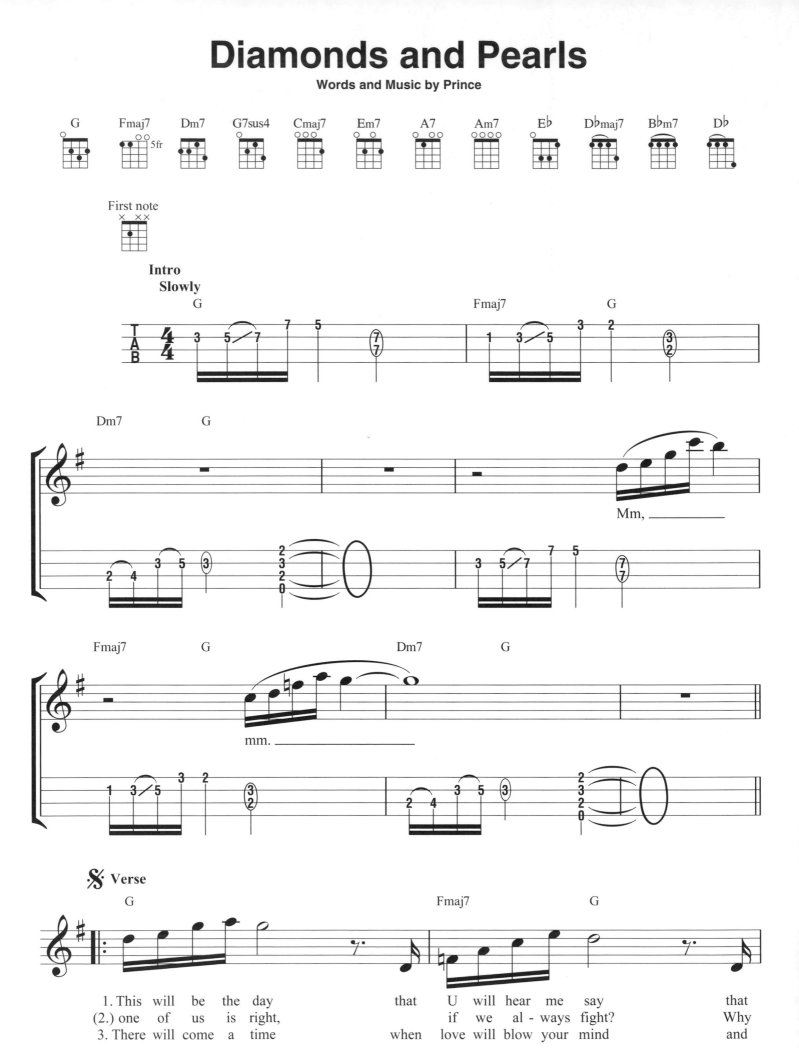

9

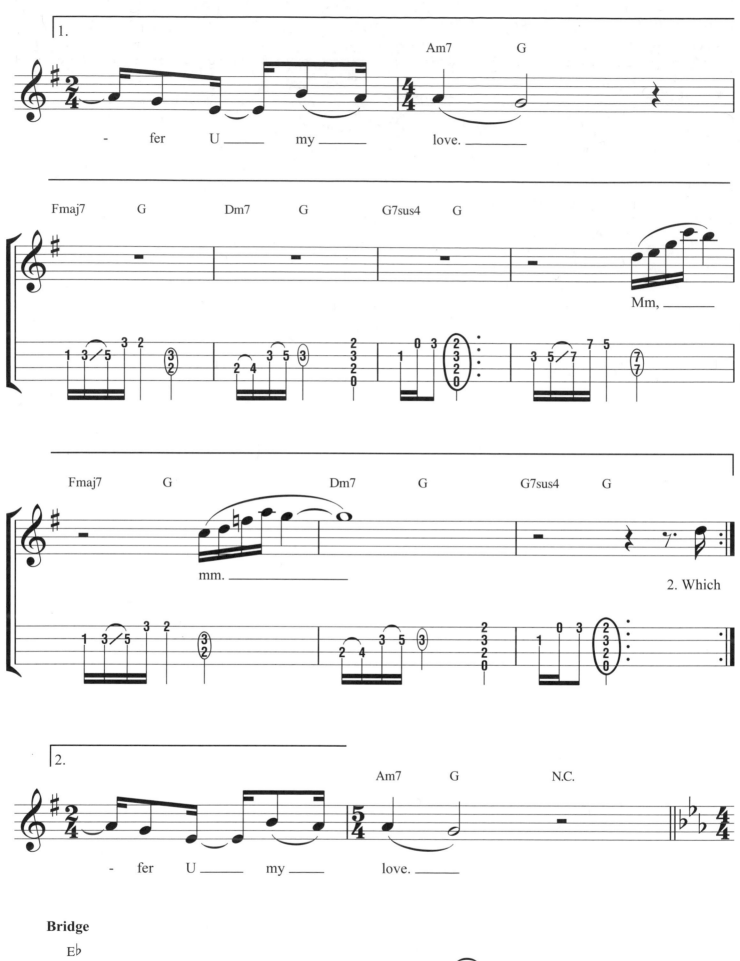

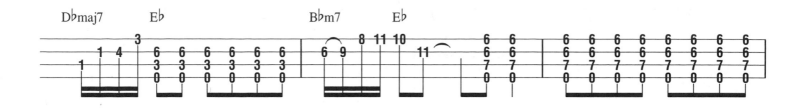

D 2 the I 2 the A 2 the M,

O 2 the N 2 the D 2 the pearls of love. ____

D 2 the I 2 the A 2 the M, _____

O 2 the N 2 the D 2 the pearls of love. ____

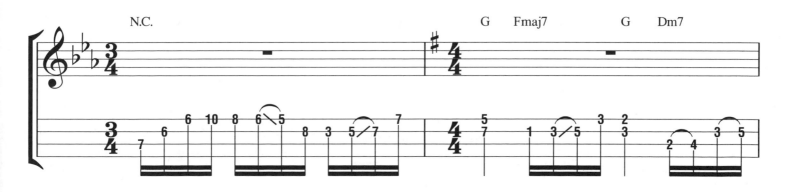

Gett Off

Words and Music by Prince and Arlester Christian

- tions in a one-night stand. Gett off. I'll __ on-ly call U

af - ter, if U say I can. _____ Gett

off. Let a wom-an be a wom-an and a man be a man. __ Gett

To Coda

1.

off. If ___ U want __ 2, ba - by... here __ I am. ___

2.

- by... here __ I am. ___

Gett off.

1, 2, ___ 3.

Bridge

N.C.(Dm)

Naw, lit - tle cut - ie, I _____ ain't drink - in'.

14

But scope this, I _____ was just think - ing: U + me, what a ride. _____

If U was think - ing the same, _____ we could con - tin - ue out -

side. Lay your pret - ty bod - y a - gainst _____ a park - in'

me - ter. Slip _____ yo dress down like I was strip - pin' a

Pe - ter Paul's Al - mond Joy. Lem - me show U, ba - by, I'm a tal - ent - ed boy. _____

D.C. al Coda

Ev - 'ry - bod - y, grab a bod - y. Pump it like U want some - bod - y.

Coda

- by... here _____ I am. _____

I Wanna Be Your Lover

Words and Music by Prince

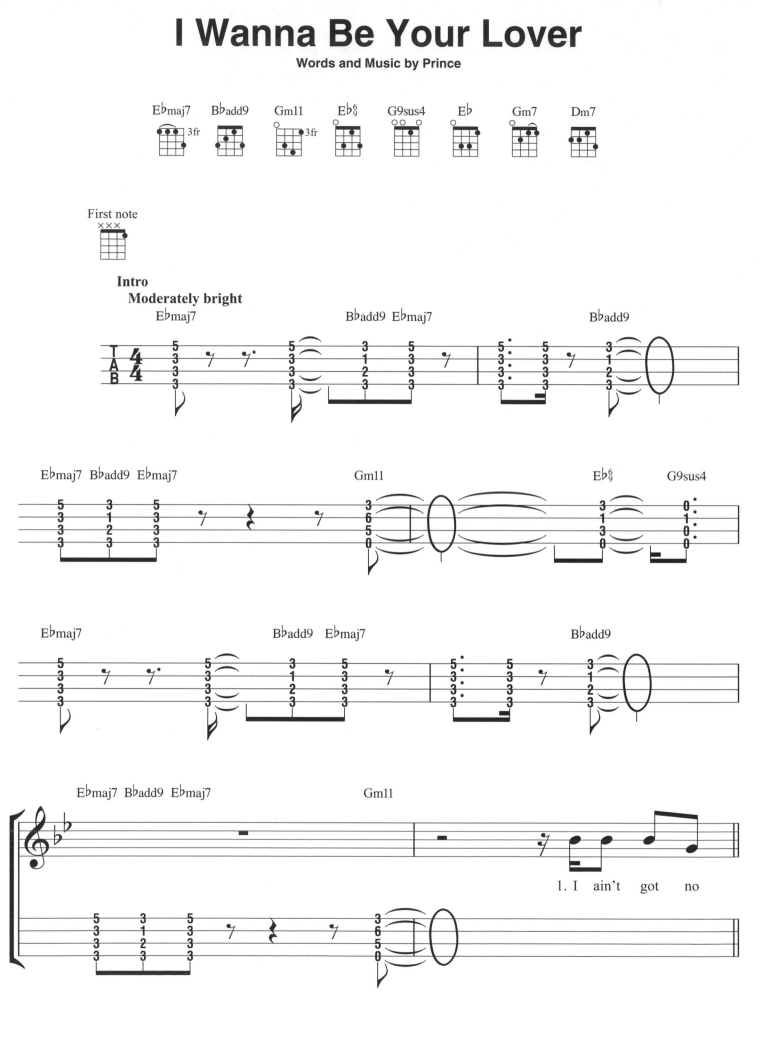

Verse

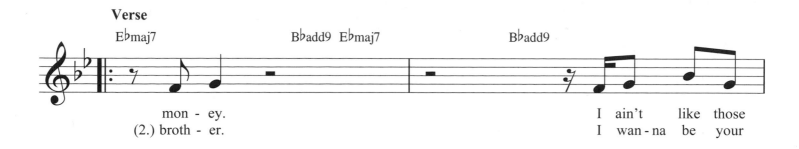

mon - ey.
(2.) broth - er.

I ain't like those
I wan - na be your

oth - er guys you hang a - round. ___
moth - er and your sis - ter, too. ___

It's kind of fun - ny,
There ain't no oth - er

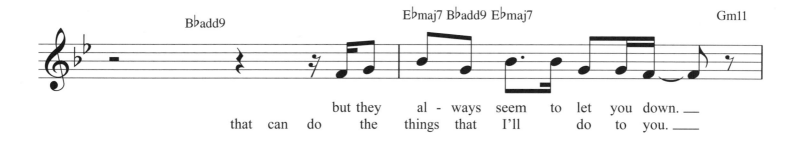

but they al - ways seem to let you down. ___
that can do the things that I'll do to you. ___

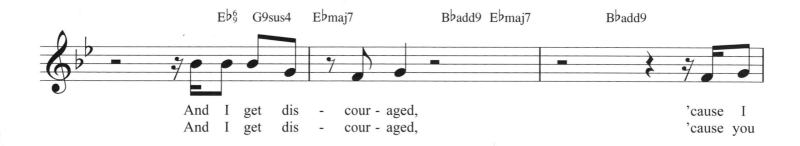

And I get dis - cour - aged,
And I get dis - cour - aged,

'cause I
'cause you

nev - er see you an - y - more. ___
treat me just like a child. ___

I need your
They say I'm

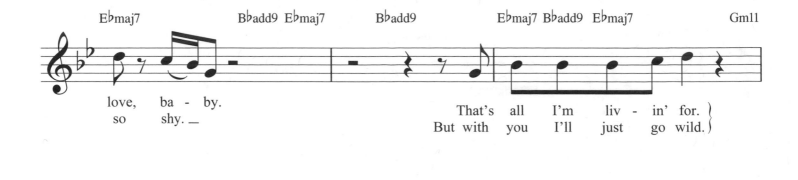

love, ba - by.
so shy. —

That's all I'm liv - in' for.
But with you I'll just go wild.

Pre-Chorus

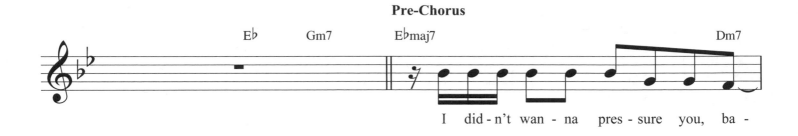

I did - n't wan - na pres - sure you, ba -

- by.   But all I ev - er want - ed to do: __

Chorus

__   I wan - na be your lov - er.

I wan-na be the on - ly one that makes you come

I Would Die 4 U

Words and Music by Prince

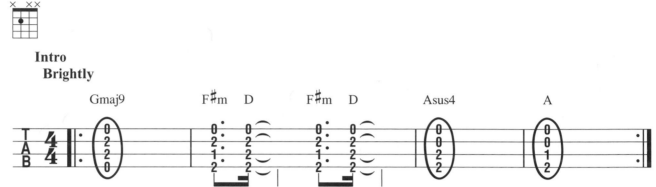

First note

Intro
Brightly

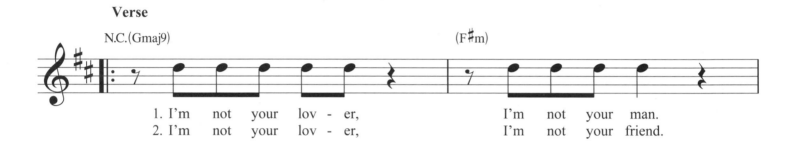

Verse

1. I'm not your lov - er, I'm not your man.
2. I'm not your lov - er, I'm not your friend.

I am some - thing that you'll nev - er un - der - stand.
I am some - thing that you'll nev - er com - pre - hend.

(Gmaj9) (F#m)

I'll nev - er beat U, I'll nev - er lie.
No need 2 wor - ry, no need 2 cry.

If you're e - vil, I'll for - give U by and by.
I'm your mes - si - ah and you're the rea - son why.

Chorus

U, I would __ die 4 ____ U,

dar - ling, if U want me 2. U,

I would __ die 4 ____ U.

Interlude

N.C.

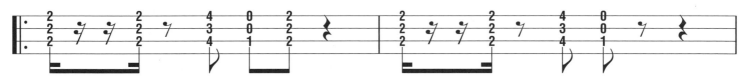

Bridge

N.C.(Gmaj9) (F#m)

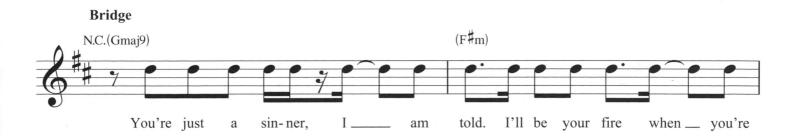

You're just a sin - ner, I ____ am told. I'll be your fire when __ you're

Kiss

Words and Music by Prince

I'm gon-na show U what it's all a-bout. _____
We could have a good time.

U don't have 2 be _____

𝄋 Chorus

rich 2 be my girl. _____ U don't have 2 be cool _____ 2 rule my world. _____

_____ Ain't no par-ti-cu-lar sign _____ I'm more com-pat-i-ble with. _____

To Coda ⊕

_____ I just want your _____ ex-tra time _____ and your

kiss. _____

1. | 2.

2. U got to not talk | 3. Wom-en, not _____

24

Let's Go Crazy

Words and Music by Prince

4 a   friend - ly   word. ___   She   just
what's   it   all   4?   U

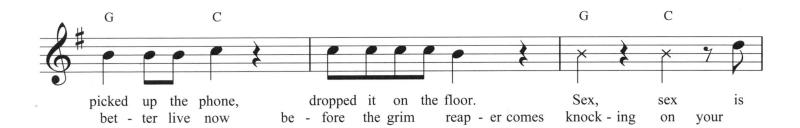

picked   up   the   phone,   dropped   it   on   the   floor.   Sex,   sex   is
bet - ter   live   now   be - fore   the   grim   reap - er   comes   knock - ing   on   your

Pre-Chorus

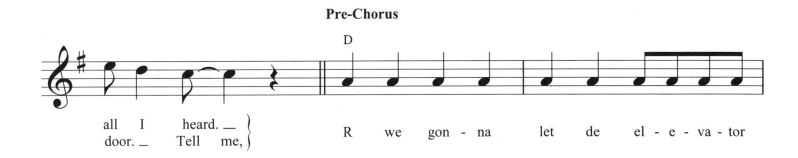

all   I   heard. ___ ⎫   R   we   gon - na   let   de   el - e - va - tor
door. ___   Tell   me, ⎭

Chorus

bring   us ___   down?   Oh   no.   Let's   go!   Let's   go   cra -

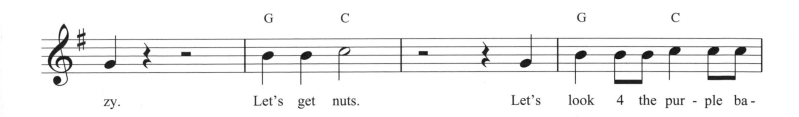

zy.   Let's   get   nuts.   Let's   look   4   the   pur - ple   ba -

Outro

He's com - ing, he's

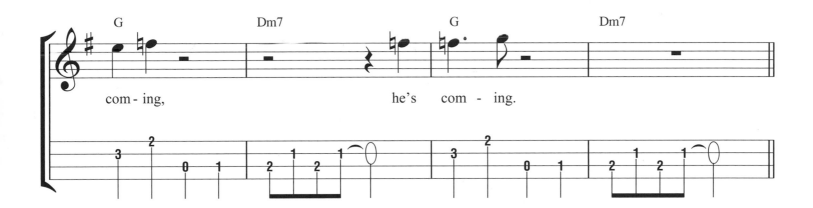

com - ing, he's com - ing.

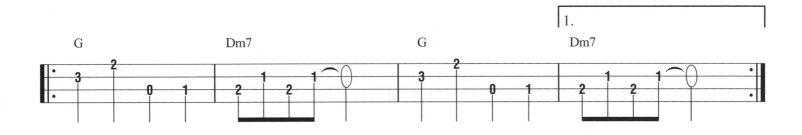

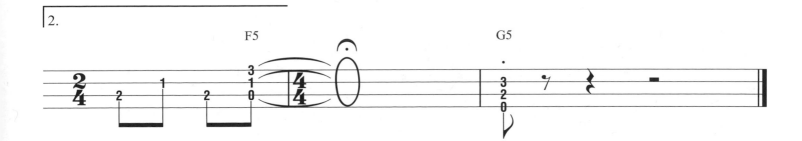

Little Red Corvette

Words and Music by Prince

Tro - jan and some of them used.
won-dered if I had e-nough class.

But it was Sat - ur - day night; _ I guess that
But it was Sat - ur - day night; _ I guess that

makes it al - right. U say, "What have I got to lose?
makes it al - right, and U say, "Ba - by, have U got e - nough gas?"

𝄋 Chorus

And, ba - by, I say:
Oh, yeah.
} Lit - tle red ___ Cor - vette,

ba - by, you're much ___ too fast. _____

Lit - tle red ___ Cor - vette,

To Coda ⊕

{ U need a love that's gon - na last.
{ got to find a love that's

1.

2.

Interlude

gon - na last, oh, oh.

Ooh, ooh, ooh.

31

1999

Words and Music by Prince

sky was all pur-ple. There were peo-ple run-nin' ev-'ry-where
War is all a-round us; my mind says pre-pare 2 fight.

try-in' 2 run from the de-struc-tion. And U
So if I got-ta die, I'm gon-na

know I did-n't e-ven care.
lis-ten 2 my bod-y 2-night.

'Cuz they say two

Chorus

thou-sand, ze-ro, ze-ro, par-ty o-ver, oops, out of time.

To Coda

So 2-night I'm gon-na par-ty like it's nine-teen nine-ty-nine.

1.

2. I was

2.

Verse

3. If U did-n't come 2 par-ty, don't both-er knock-in' on my door.

Money Don't Matter 2 Night

Words and Music by Prince

Bm7   Cmaj7   Dm7

First note

Intro
Moderately

1. One more card and it's 2 _____ 2, un-
2. Look, here's a cool in - vest - ment. They're
3. Hey now, may - be we can find a good rea - son 2

luck - y 4 him a - gain. He nev - er had re - spect 4
tell - in' him he just can't lose. So he goes off and tries 2
send a child off 2 _____ war. So what if we're con - trol - lin'

mon - ey, it's true, _____ that's why he nev - er wins. _____ That's
find a part - ner, _____ but all he finds _____ are us - ers.
all the oil, _____ is it worth the child dy - ing 4? _____ If

why he nev - er ev - er has _____ e - nough _____ 2 treat his la - dy right.
All he finds are snakes in ev - er - y col - or, ev - er - y na - tion - al - i - ty and size. _____
long life is what we all _____ live 4, _____ then long life will come to pass. _____

_____ He just push - es her a - way in a huff _____ and says
_____ Seems like the on - ly thing that he can do _____ is just
_____ An - y - thing is bet - ter than the pic - ture of a child in a

Raspberry Beret

Words and Music by Prince

told me sev - 'ral times that he did - n't like my kind ___ 'cause
put her on the back of my bike and we went rid - ing ___

I was a bit 2 ___ lei - sure - ly. ___ He
down by old man John - son's farm. ___

seen that I was bus - y do - ing some - thing close 2 noth - ing but
O - ver - cast days nev - er turned me on, but

dif - f'rent from the day be - fore. ___ That's when I saw her,
some - thing a - bout the clouds and her mixed. She was - n't 2 bright, but

Ow, I saw her. She walked in through the out door, out door. ⎫ She wore a
I could tell when she kissed me she knew how 2 get her kicks. ⎭

Chorus

rasp - ber - ry be - ret ___ of the kind U find ___ in a

sec - ond - hand   store.   Rasp - ber - ry   be - ret, _____   and

if   it   was   warm, ___   she   would - n't   wear   much   more.

Rasp - ber - ry   be - ret; _____   I   think   I

love _____   her.

Bridge

(Spoken:) The   rain   feels   so   cool   when   it   hits   the   barn   roof

and   the   horses   wonder   who   U   are.

Thunder drowns out what the lightning sees. U

feel like a movie star.

They say the first time ain't the greatest, but

if I had the chance 2 do it all again, I

would-n't change a stroke, 'cause, ba-by, I'm the most with a

girl as fine as she was then. _____ She wore a

Chorus

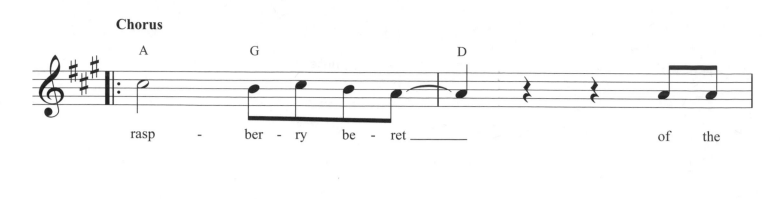

raspberry beret _____ of the

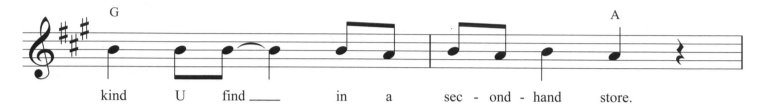

kind U find ____ in a second-hand store.

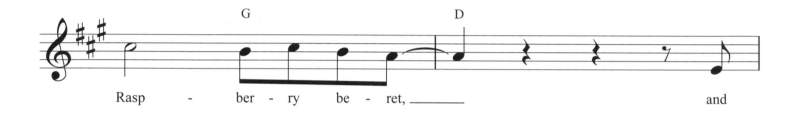

Raspberry beret, _____ and

if it was warm, ___ she wouldn't wear much more.

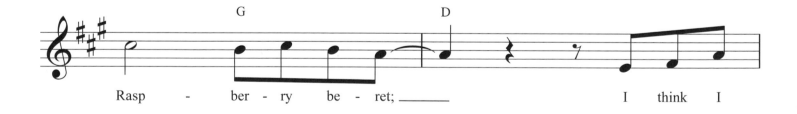

Raspberry beret; _____ I think I

Repeat and fade

love _____ her. She wore a

Purple Rain

Words and Music by Prince

1.

B♭add9 N.C.

rain.   2. I   nev - er want-ed   2   be   your   week - end   lov -

2.

D.C. al Coda

B♭add9   N.C.

3

rain.   3. Hon - ey,   I   know,   I   know, ___   I   know   times   r

⊕ **Coda**

On - ly   wan - na   see   U, ___

B♭add9

___   on - ly   wan - na   see   U ___   in   the   pur - ple   rain.

Additional Lyrics

2. I never wanted 2 be your weekend lover.
   I only wanted 2 be some kind of friend.
   Baby, I could never steal U from another.
   It's such a shame our friendship had 2 end.

3. Honey, I know, I know, I know times r changing.
   It's time we all reach out 4 something new. That means you, too.
   U say U want a leader, but U can't seem 2 make up your mind.
   I think U better close it and let me guide U 2 the purple rain.

Sign o' the Times

Words and Music by Prince

soon she did the same. ____ At home, ____ there are sev-en-teen-year - old boys, ____ and

their _ i - de - a of fun _____ is be-ing in a gang called _ the Dis-ci - ples, high _

____ on crack, _____ and tot - in' a ma - chine gun. ____

Chorus

N.C.(C5)

Time, _____ time. ____

2. Hur -

Verse

N.C.(C5)

-ri-cane An-nie ripped the ceil-ing off a church and killed ___

_____ ev-'ry-one in-side. _____ U turn on the tel-ly and ev - 'ry oth-er sto-ry is tell-

-in' U some-bod-y died. _____ Sis-

-ter killed her ba-by cuz she could-n't af-ford ___ 2 feed ___

___ it, and we're send-ing peo - ple 2 the moon.

In Sep-tem-ber, my cous - in tried reef-er 4 the ver-y first time; now he's do-ing horse.

Chorus

N.C.(C5)

It's June. ___

Times, _____ times. __

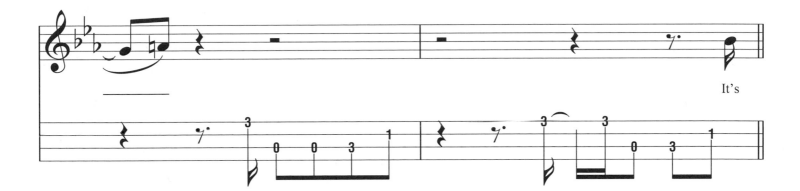

_____ It's

Bridge

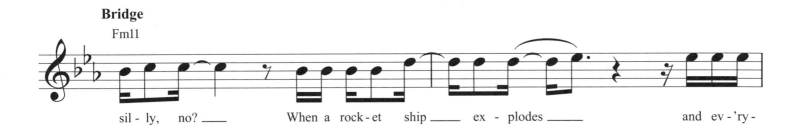

Fm11

sil - ly, no? ____ When a rock - et ship ____ ex - plodes ____ and ev - 'ry-

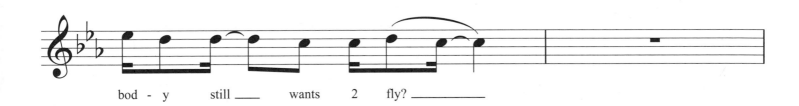

bod - y still ____ wants 2 fly? ____

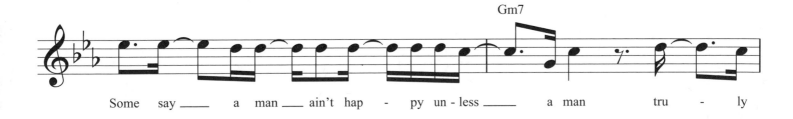

Gm7

Some say ____ a man ____ ain't hap - py un - less ____ a man tru - ly

Fm11   Gm7

dies. _____ Oh, ____ why? _____

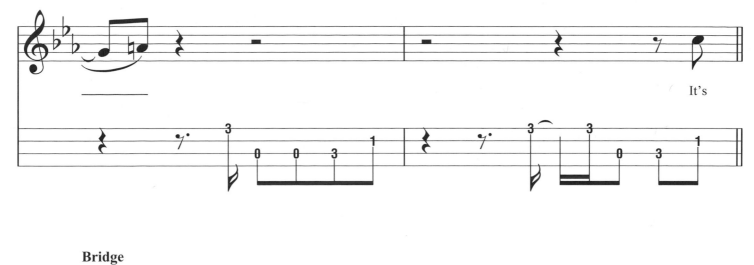

It's

Bridge

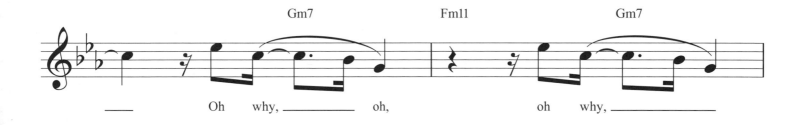

sil-ly, _____ when a rock-et blows _ and ev-'ry-bod-y still _ wants _ 2 fly.

Some say man ain't hap-py, tru - ly, 'til man tru - ly dies. _

_ Oh why, _____ oh, oh why, _____

sign _____ o' _____ the times.

Chorus

N.C.(C5)

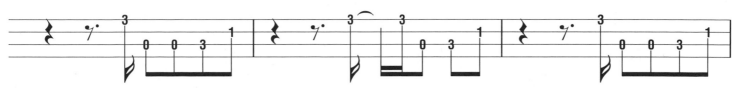

Time, _____

time.

Outro

N.C.(C5)

Sign o' the times ____ mess ____ with your mind, ____ hur -

- ry be - fore ____ it's 2 late. ____ Let's

fall in love, _____ get mar - ried, have a ba - by.

We'll call him Nate (if it's a boy.)

Time, _____ time. _____

Repeat and fade

Thieves in the Temple

Words and Music by Prince

Verse

1. Love, if U're there, come save me from all ___ this cold de - spair. _

___ I can hang ___ when U're a - round, ___ but I'll

sure - ly die if U're not there. ___ Love, come ___ quick.

Love, come ___ in a hur - ry. There are

thieves ___ in the tem - ple 2 - night.

I feel ___ like they're look - in' 4 my soul, ___ like a

poor man look-in' 4 ____ gold. ____ There are thieves in the

tem - ple 2 - night. ____

Verse

Cm7   Gm

2. Voic-es from the sky say re - ly on your best friend 2 pull ya thru. ____

Cm7

But e - ven if I want-ed 2, I could - n't real - ly tru - ly cuz my

Chorus

D   N.C.   Gm7

on - ly friend is U, oo.   There are

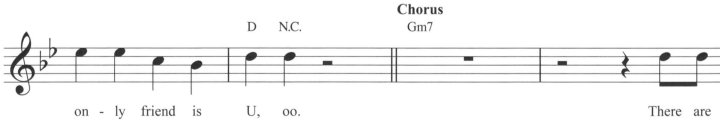

thieves ____ in the tem - ple 2 - night,

kick - in' me ___ in ___ my ___ heart, ___

tear - in' me all ___ a - part, ___ cuz me and U ___ could have

been a work ___ of art. (Thieves in the tem - ple.) Ba - by, don't U

Bridge

Gm ___ Gm(maj7) ___ Gm7 ___ C7 ___ Gm ___ Gm(maj7)

know I'm hold - in' on the best that I can. ___ Love, _ please ___ help me 2 be the

Gm7 ___ C7 ___ Cm7 ___ D ___ N.C.

bet - ter ___ man, ___ bet - ter than the thieves ___ in the tem - ple, in the tem - ple 2 -

D.S. al Coda ___ Coda

Gm7 ___ D+

night. ___ tem - ple 2 - night.

U Got the Look

Words and Music by Prince

U sho-'nuff do be cook-in' in my book. Your face is jam- min',

your bod-y's heck-a-slam-min'! If love is good, let's get 2 ram- min'.

To Coda 2 **To Coda 1**

U got the look. U got the look.

Verse

2. U got the look. U must-a took a whole ho-ur just 2

make up your face, ba - by. Clos-in' time, ug - ly lights,

ev -'ry-bod - y's in-spect-ed. But U are a nat'ral beau-ty

un - af - fect - ed. *Did I say an hour? My face is red.*

D.S. al Coda 1 **Coda 1** ***D.S.S. al Coda 2*** **Coda 2**

I stand corrected. 3. U walked

When Doves Cry

Words and Music by Prince

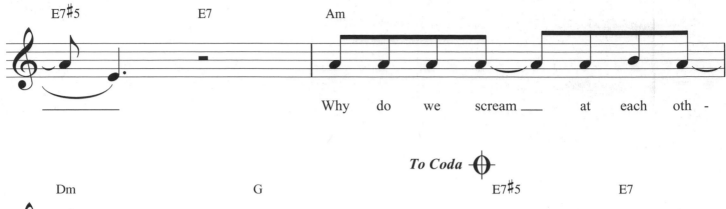

Why do we scream ___ at each oth -

- er? This is what it sounds like when doves ___ cry.

Interlude

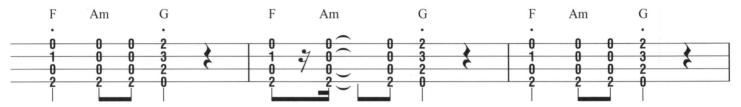

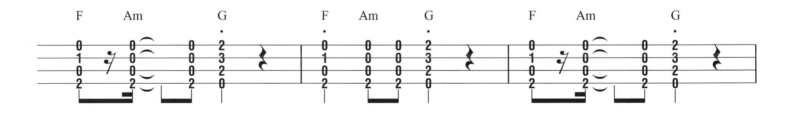

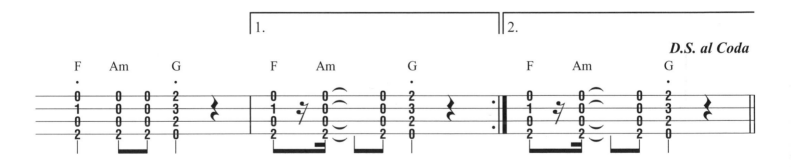

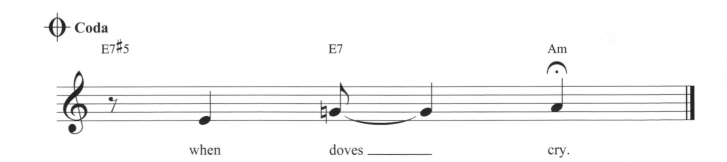

when doves _____ cry.